Date: 7/27/12

Published by Creative Education
P.O. Box 227, Mankato, Minnesota 56002
Creative Education is an imprint of
The Creative Company
www.thecreativecompany.us

Design and production by The Design Lab
Art direction by Rita Marshall
Printed by Corporate Graphics in the
United States of America

Photographs by Alamy (Arco Images GmbH),
Corbis (Norbert Wu/Science Faction), Dreamstime
(Glen Gaffney, Todd Gantzler), Getty Images (David
B. Fleetham, Tyson Mackay), iStockphoto (Jami
Garrison, John Gaudette, Brian Gudas, Tatiana
Ivkovich, Hakan Karlsson, Michael Kempf)

Library of Congress Cataloging-in-Publication Data
Riggs, Kate.
Killer whales / by Kate Riggs.
p. cm. — (Amazing animals)
Summary: A basic exploration of the appearance,
behavior, and habitat of killer whales, Earth's
deadliest dolphins. Also included is a story from
folklore explaining the killer whale's creation.
Includes bibliographical references and index.
ISBN 978-1-60818-109-4
1. Killer whale—Juvenile literature. I. Title.
QL737.C432R554 2012
599.53'6—dc22   2010049129

CPSIA: 011212 PO1521

9 8 7 6 5 4 3 2

AMAZING ANIMALS
KILLER WHALES

BY KATE RIGGS

CREATIVE EDUCATION

A killer whale pops above the water to look for food

A killer whale is a big animal that lives in the ocean. There is only one kind of killer whale. It is found in the coldest ocean waters around the world.

ocean a big area of deep, salty water

Killer whales have skin that is black and white. They have a thick layer of fat called blubber under their skin. The fat helps a killer whale stay warm in the cold water. A killer whale has a tail and two flippers to help it swim.

A killer whale's tail has two pads called flukes (above)

A male killer whale weighs up to 12,000 pounds (5,443 kg). A female weighs about 8,000 pounds (3,629 kg). Killer whales grow to be 16 to 26 feet (4.8–8 m) long. They can swim up to 30 miles (48 km) per hour.

Killer whales are heavy, but they can jump out of the water

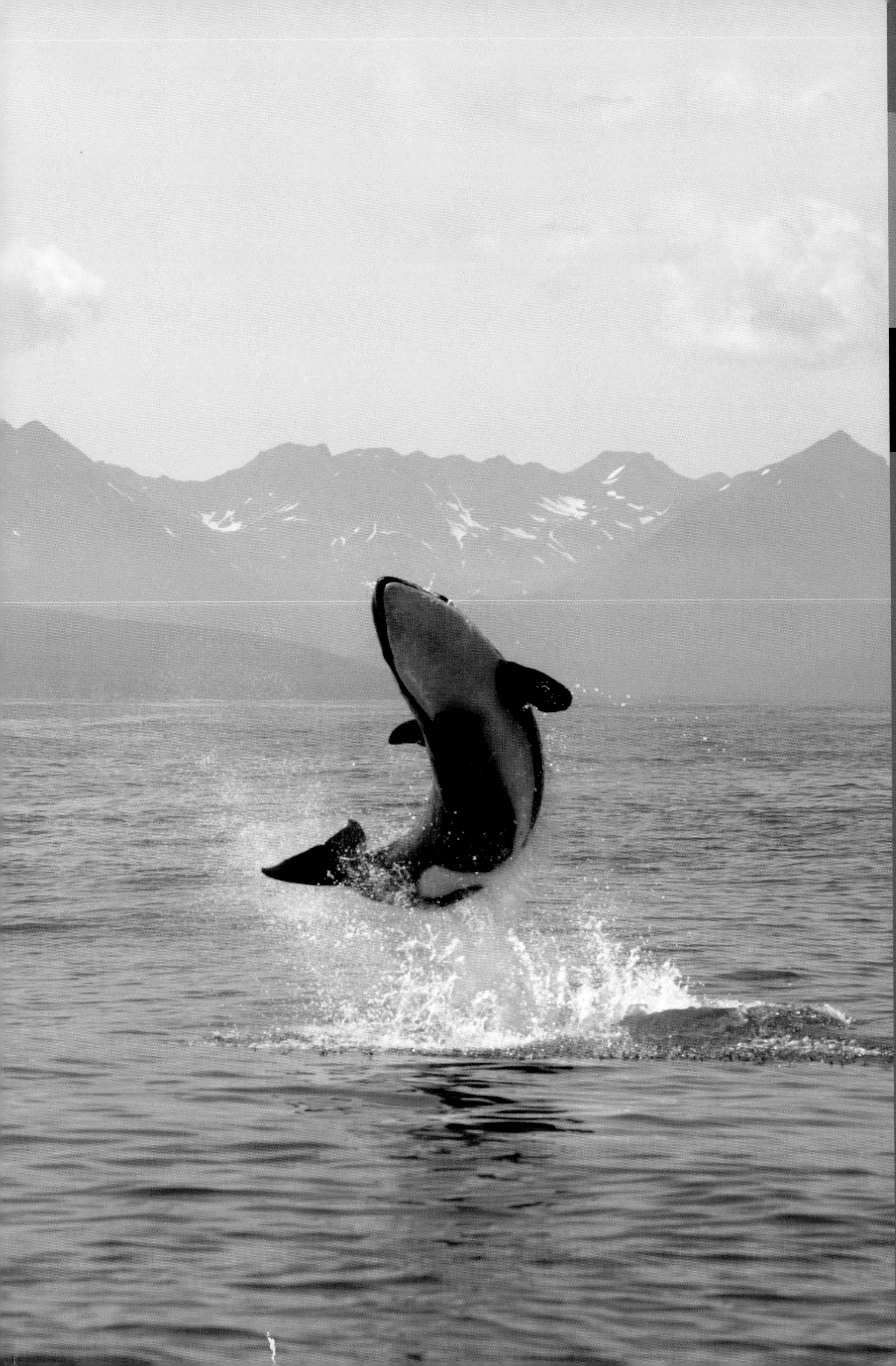

The blowhole opens when a killer whale comes to the surface

Killer whales live near the coldest parts of the world. They stay in the water all the time, but they need to breathe air. They breathe through a **blowhole**.

blowhole a hole in the skin on top of a killer whale's head that opens to take in air

Killer whales eat meat. They like eating fish, penguins, sea lions, and seals. They also eat big animals called walruses. Walruses can weigh 4,000 pounds (1,814 kg)!

Killer whales sometimes work together to catch walruses (above)

A calf knows how to swim
as soon as it is born

A mother killer whale has one **calf** at a time. A calf drinks its mother's milk to grow big and strong. It starts eating meat when it is about four months old. A calf gains 1,000 pounds (454 kg) in its first year. Wild killer whales can live for 60 or 70 years.

calf a baby killer whale

Killer whale families live in groups called pods. There are 10 to 20 killer whales in a pod. One female leads the pod. Some pods **migrate** to follow **prey**. Other pods stay in the same area for a long time.

migrate to move from place to place during different parts of the year

prey animals that are killed and eaten by other animals

The killer whales in a pod "talk" to each other using many sounds. They make clicks, whistles, squeaks, and pops. Their whistles sound like songs. Killer whales talk to each other a lot.

Killer whales talk underwater but not while leaping

Most people know about killer whales from movies and zoos. They go to places such as SeaWorld to see a famous killer whale named Shamu. People like to watch these big animals swim and play!

A killer whale is about 65 times larger than an adult man

A Killer Whale Story

How did the killer whale come to be? People in Canada used to tell a story about this. There was once a great hunter of sea lions. One day, his boat tipped over. Some sea lions saved him. They gave him a magical knife. The hunter used the knife to carve a large creature out of a tree. It became a killer whale when it touched the water. The killer whale took the hunter home and watched over him.

Read More

Morgan, Sally. *Orcas and Other Cold-Ocean Life*. Mankato, Minn.: QEB Publishing, 2009.

Pryor, Kimberley Jane. *Icy Seas*. North Mankato, Minn.: Smart Apple Media, 2008.

Web Sites

Animal Planet: Killer Whale Facts, Pictures, Video
http://animal.discovery.com/mammals/orca/
This site has videos of killer whales to watch and a puzzle to put together.

National Geographic Kids Creature Feature: Killer Whales
http://kids.nationalgeographic.com/kids/animals/creaturefeature/orca/
This site has pictures and videos of killer whales.

Index